FOR ORGANS, PIANOS & ELECTRONIC KEYBOARDS

E·Z PLAY® TODAY

167

B ach

T0068341

ISBN 978-1-4950-3469-5

HAL·LEONARD®
CORPORATION

7777 W. BLUEMOUND RD. P.O. BOX 13819 MILWAUKEE, WI 53213

Visit Hal Leonard Online at
www.halleonard.com

Contents

4

Air on the G String
from ORCHESTRAL SUITE NO. 3

Registration 3
Rhythm: Ballad or None

By Johann Sebastian Bach

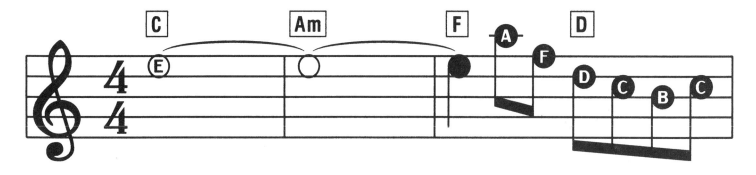

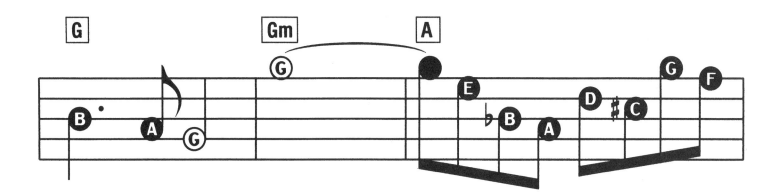

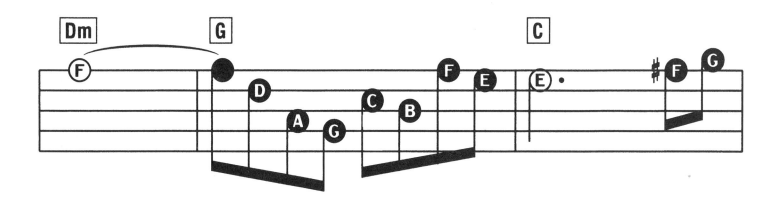

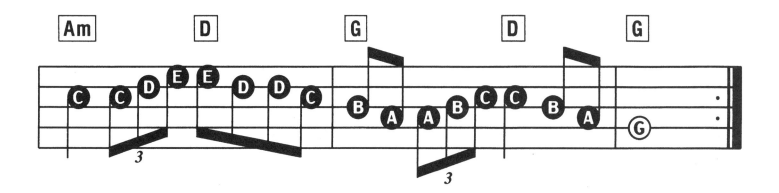

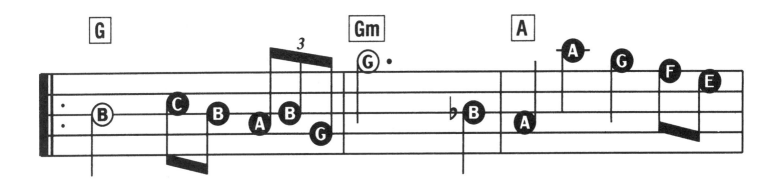

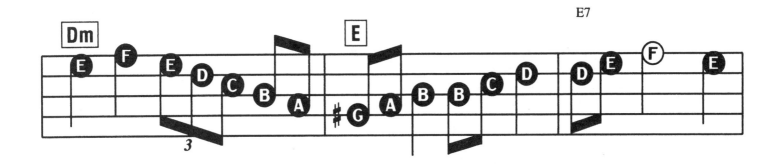

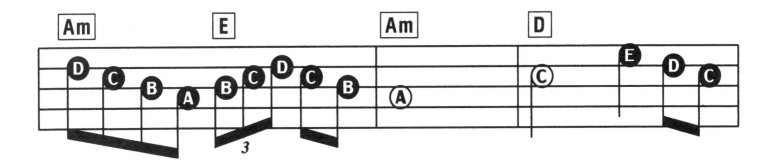

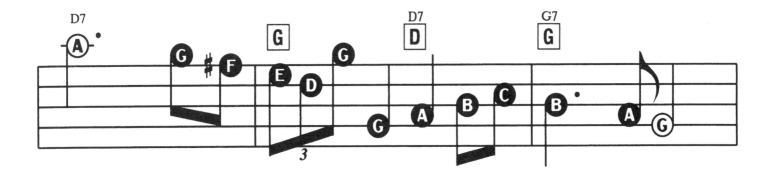

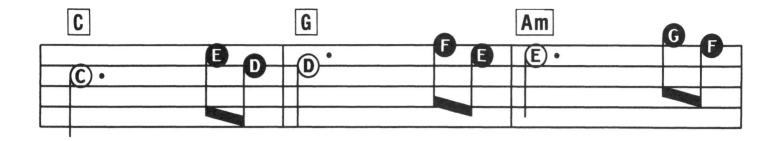

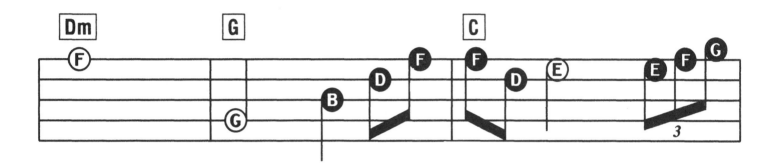

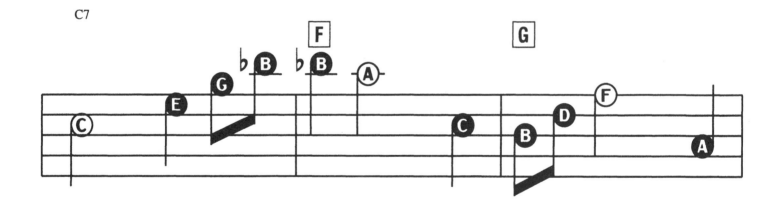

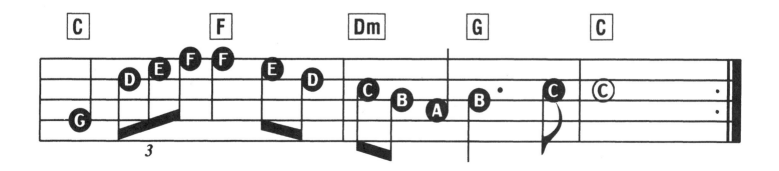

Ave Maria
based on "Prelude in C Major" by Johann Sebastian Bach

Registration 7
Rhythm: None

By Charles Gounod

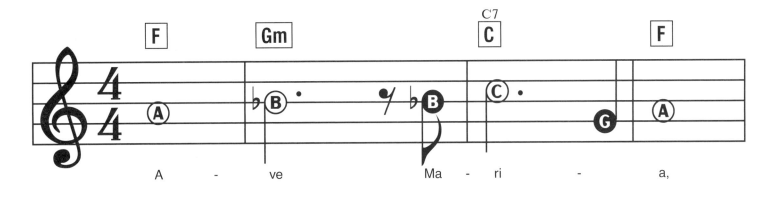

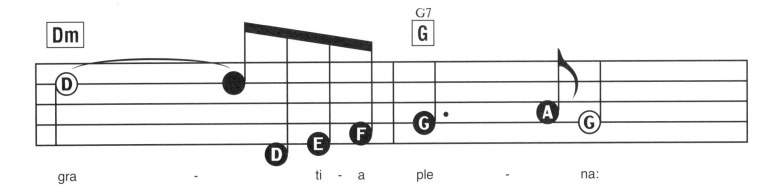

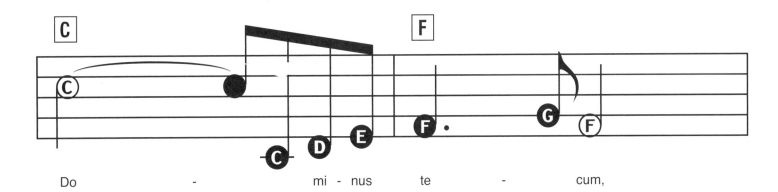

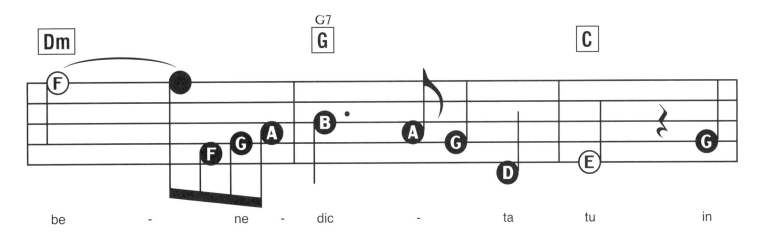

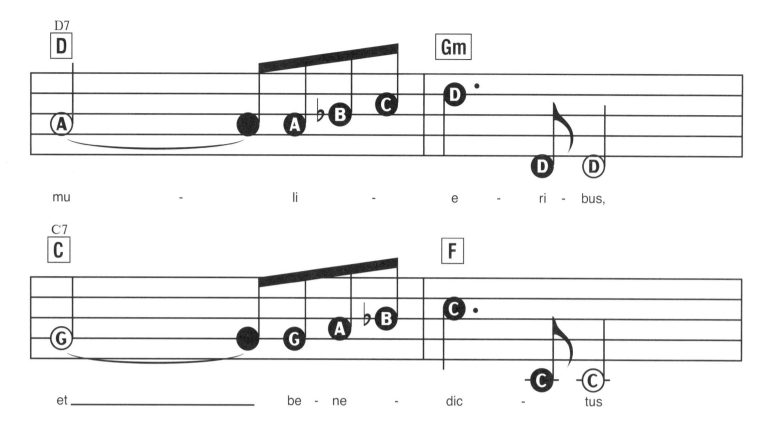

mu - li - e - ri - bus,

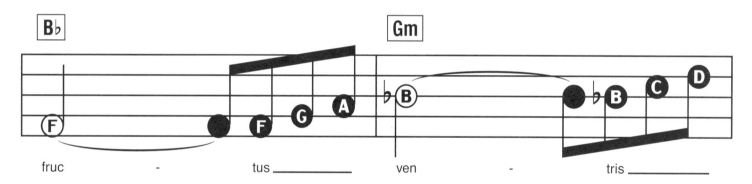

et _____ be - ne - dic - tus

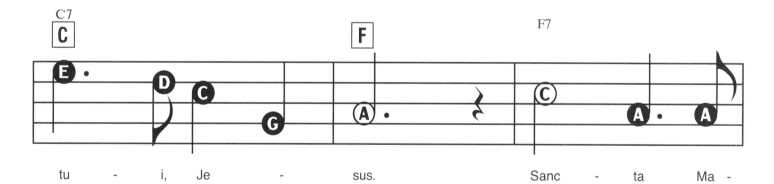

fruc - tus _____ ven - tris _____

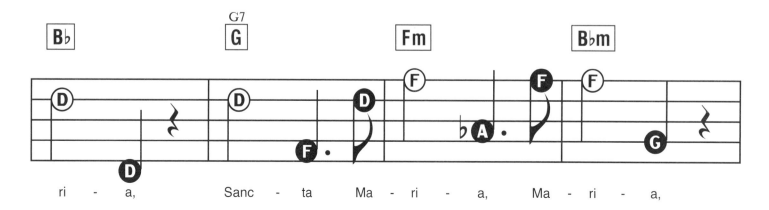

tu - i, Je - sus.   Sanc - ta Ma -

ri - a,   Sanc - ta Ma - ri - a, Ma - ri - a,

9

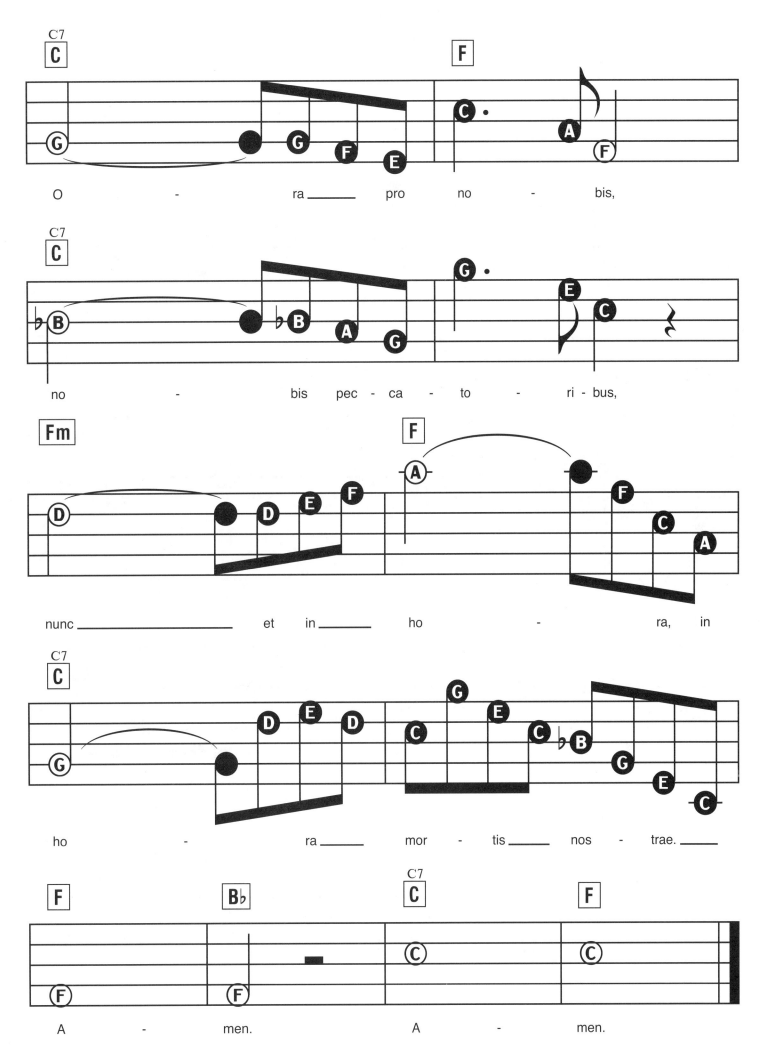

Arioso
from CANTATA NO. 156

Registration 3
Rhythm: 8-beat

By Johann Sebastian Bach

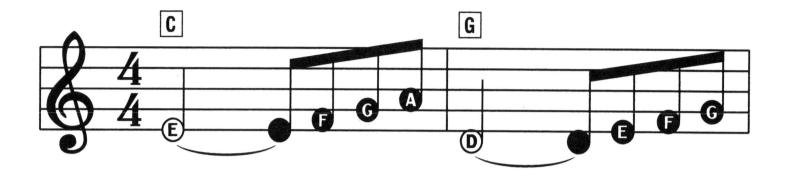

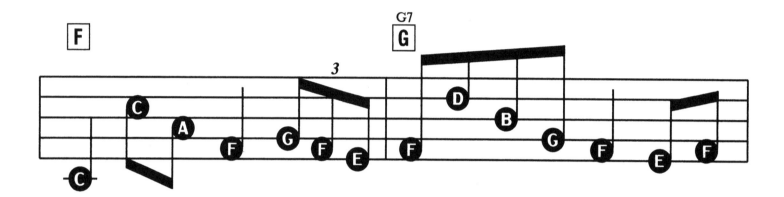

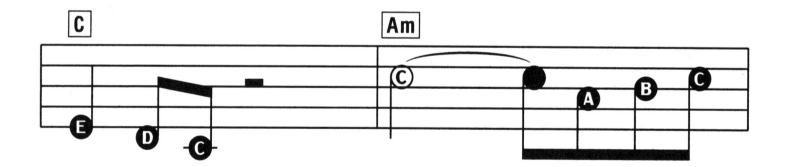

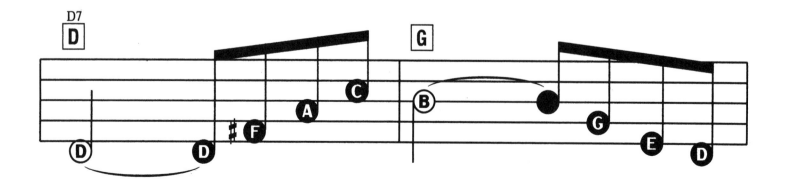

11

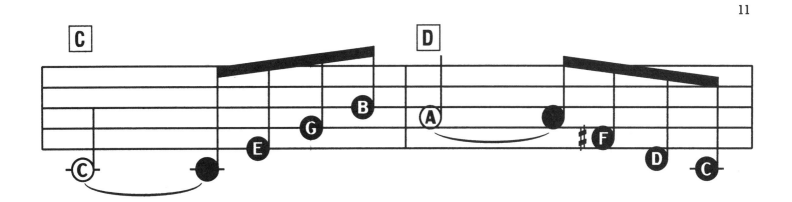

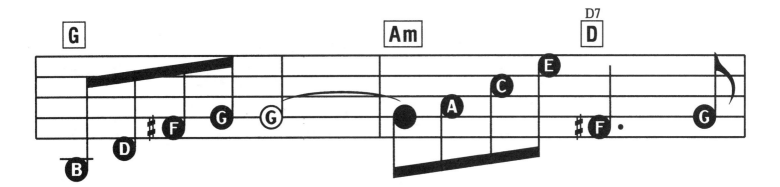

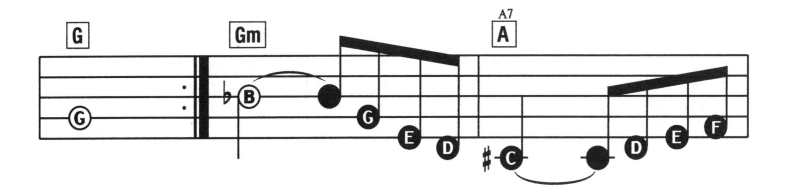

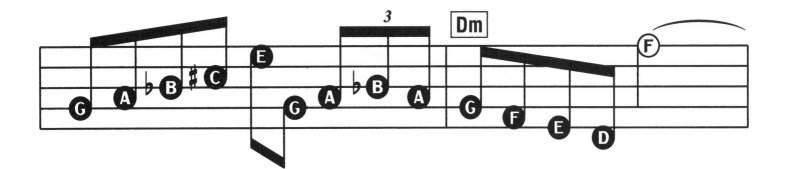

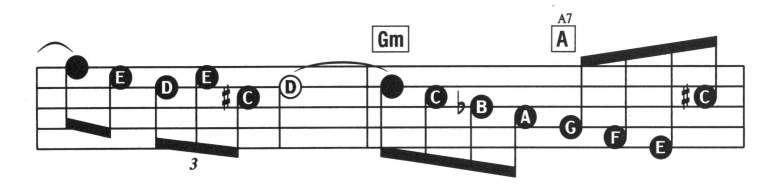

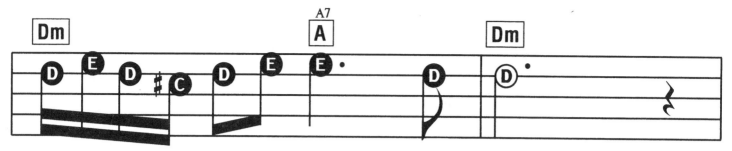

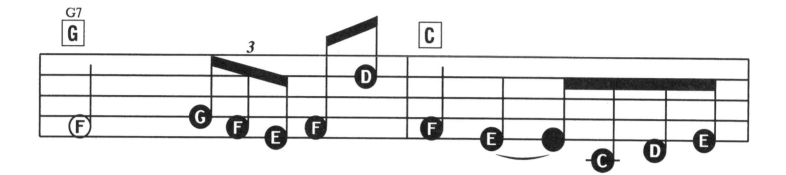

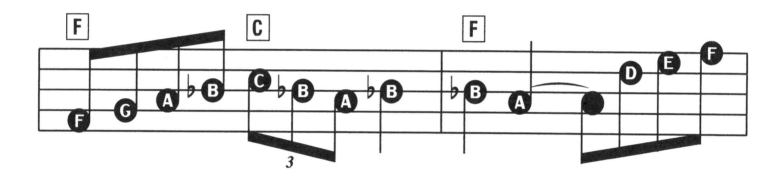

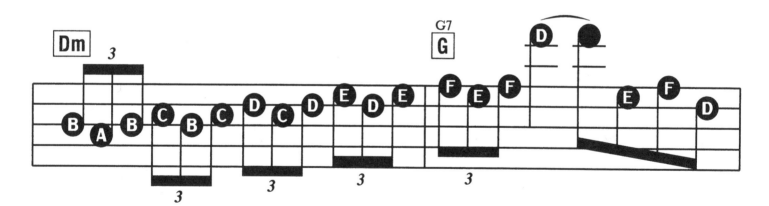

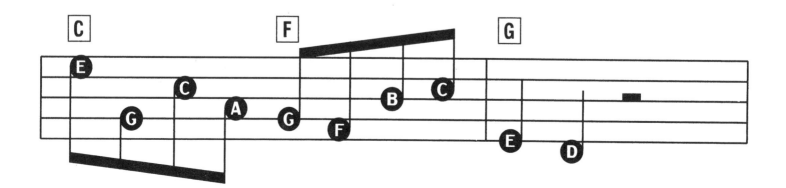

13

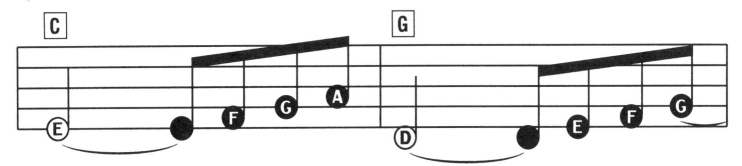

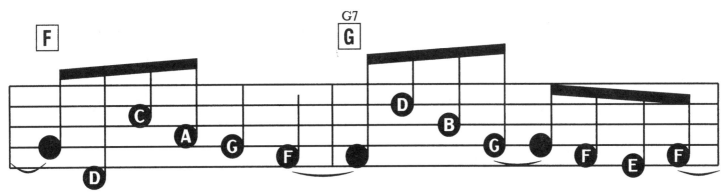

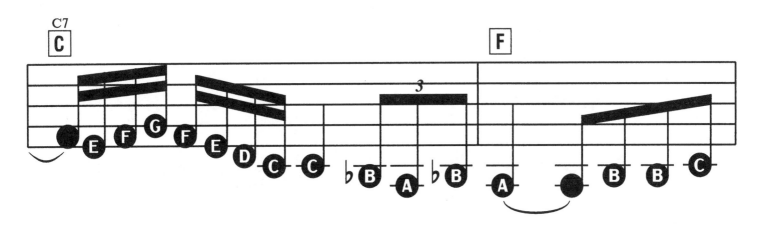

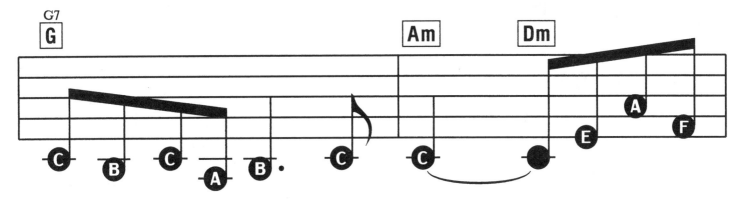

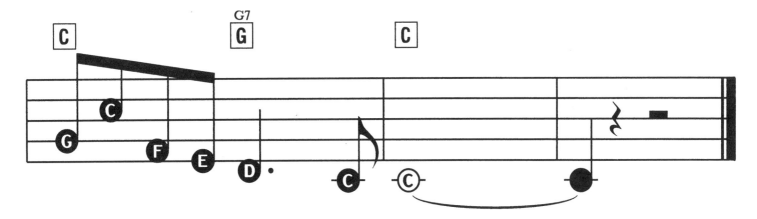

Badinerie
from ORCHESTRAL SUITE NO. 2

Registration 1
Rhythm: Fox Trot or None

By Johann Sebastian Bach

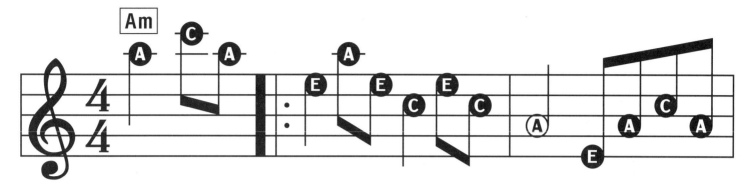

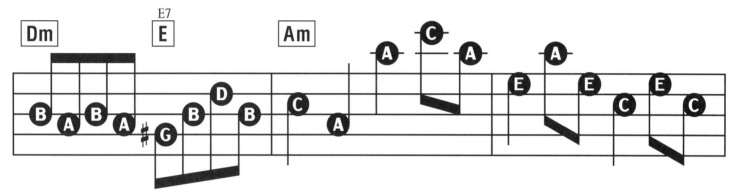

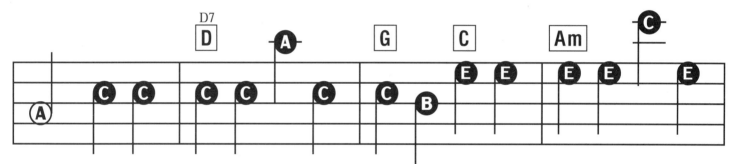

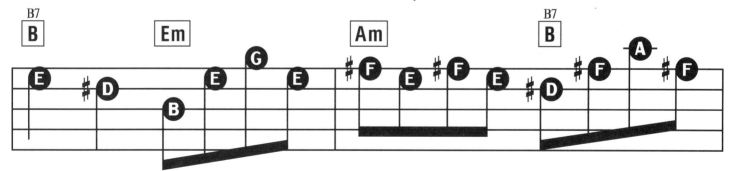

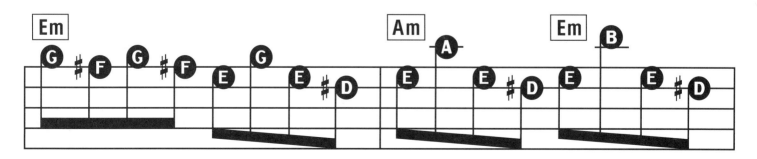

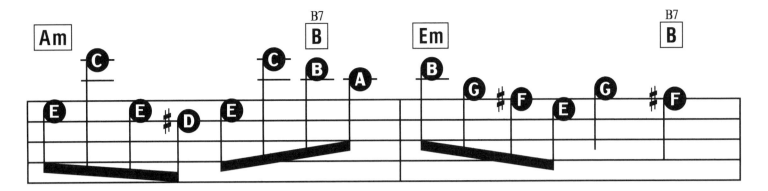

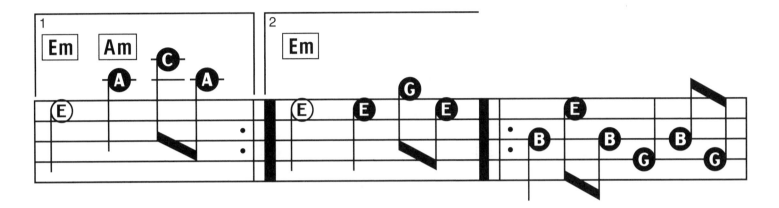

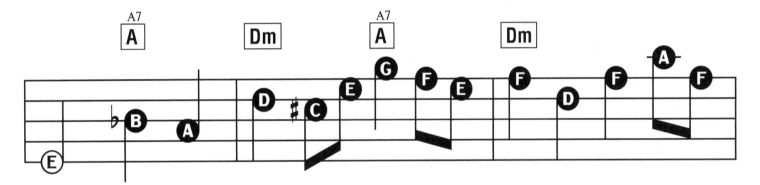

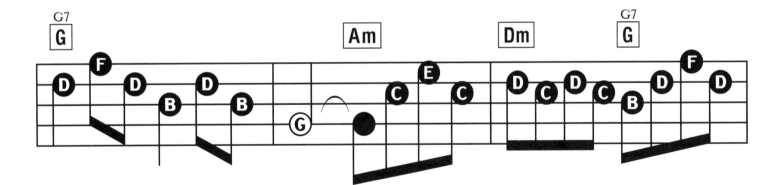

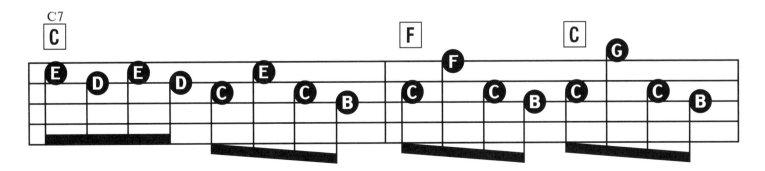

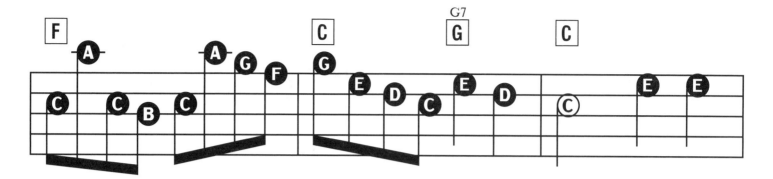

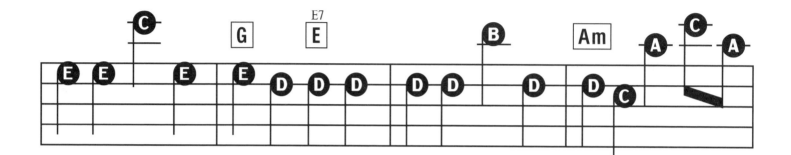

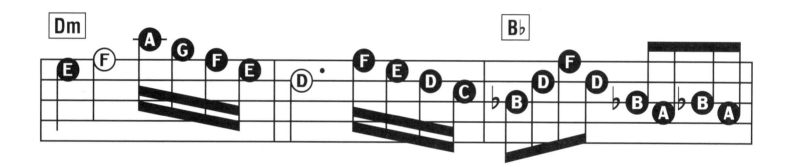

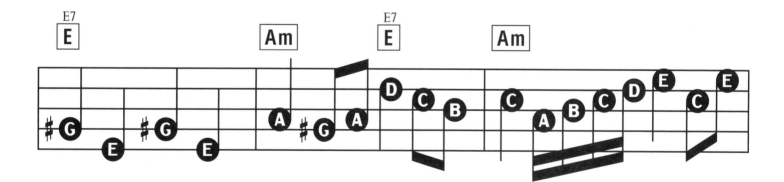

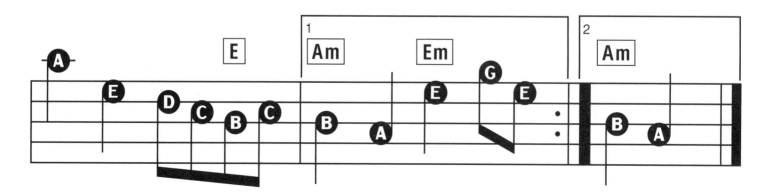

Bist du bei mir
(You Are with Me)

Registration 3
Rhythm: Waltz or None

By Johann Sebastian Bach

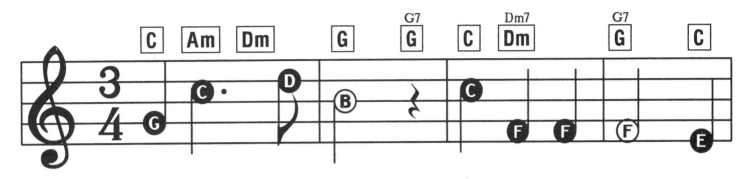

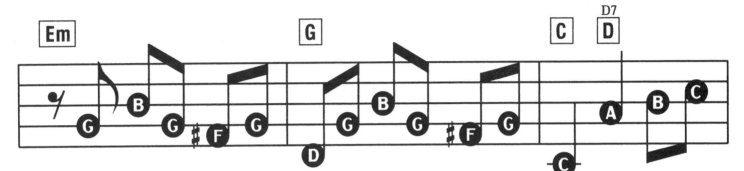

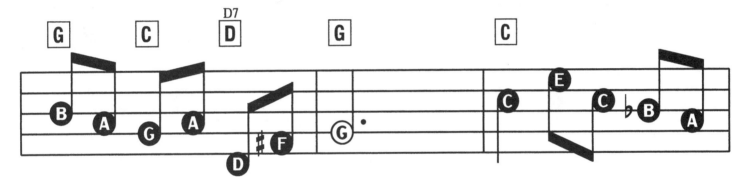

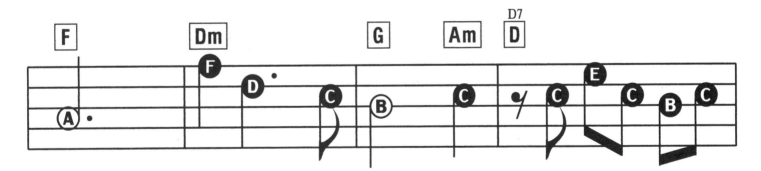

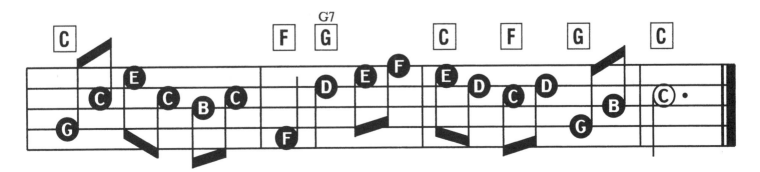

Break Forth, O Beauteous Heavenly Light
from THE CHRISTMAS ORATORIO

Words by Johann Rist
Translated by Rev. J. Troutbeck
Melody by Johann Schop
Arranged by Johann Sebastian Bach

Registration 4
Rhythm: March

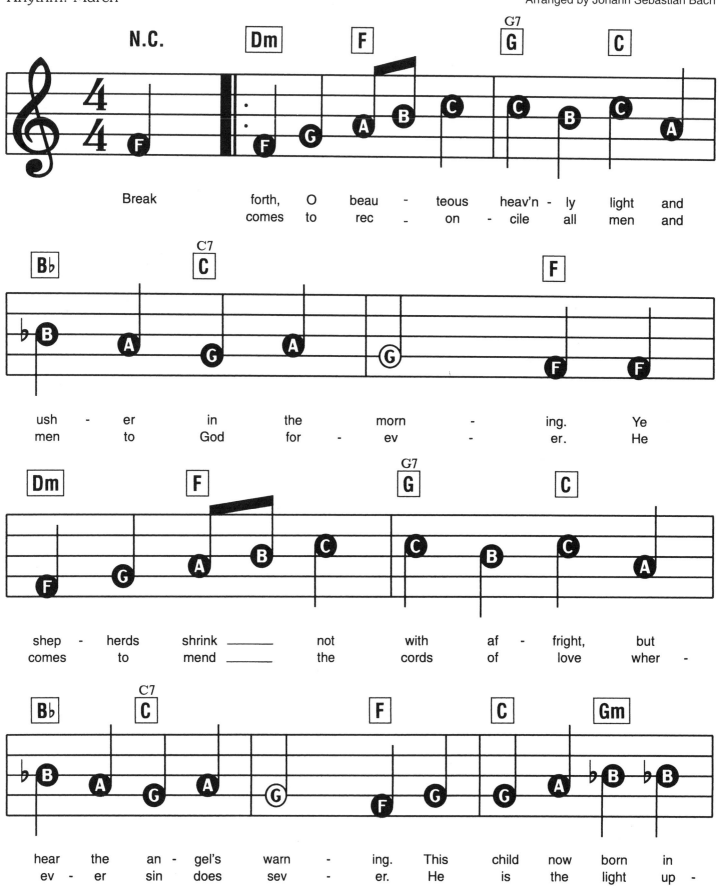

Break forth, O beau - teous heav'n - ly light and
comes to rec - on - cile all men and

ush - er in the morn - ing. Ye
men to God the for - ev - er. He

shep - herds shrink ____ not with af - fright, but
comes to mend ____ the cords of love wher -

hear the an - gel's warn - ing. This child now born in
ev - er sin does sev - er. He is the light up -

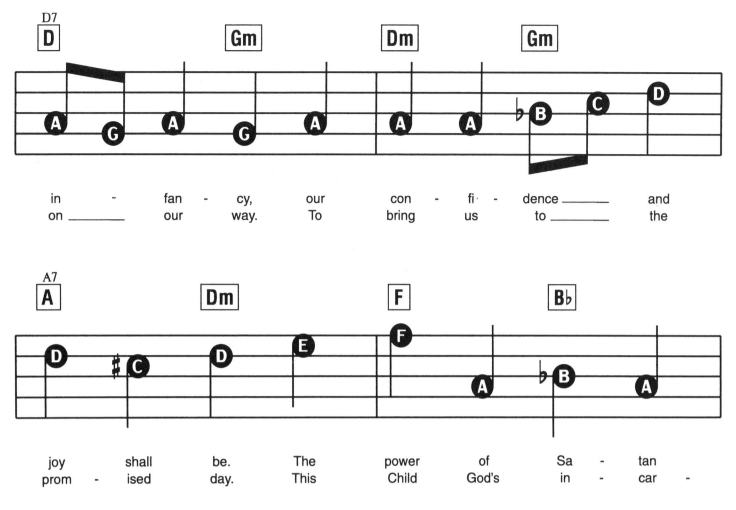

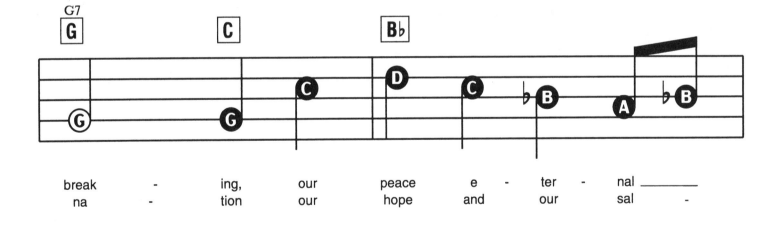

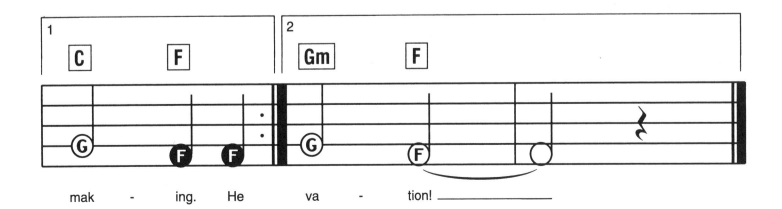

Fugue in G Minor ("Little")

Registration 6
Rhythm: March or None

By Johann Sebastian Bach

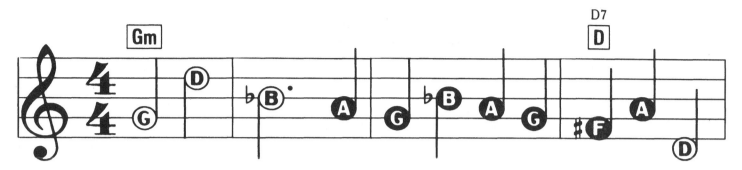

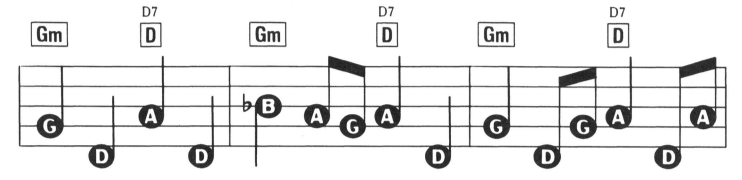

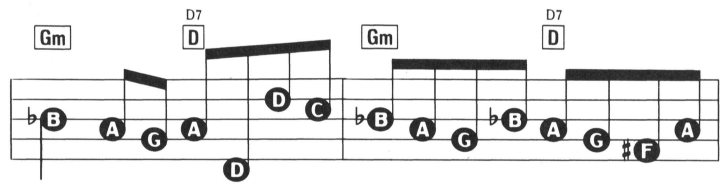

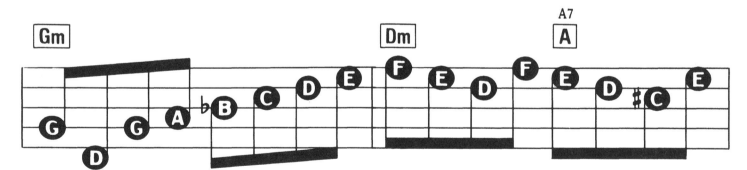

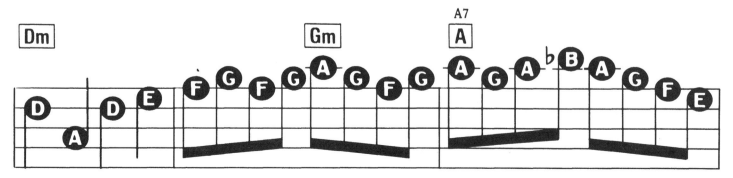

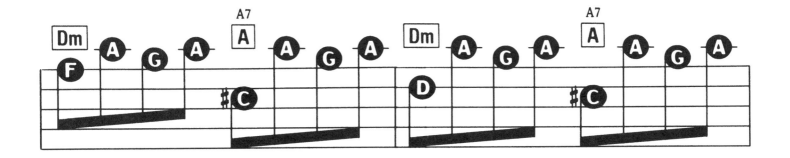

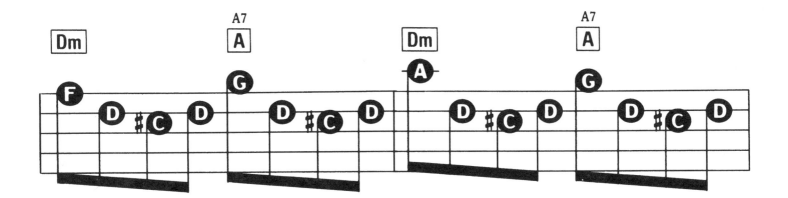

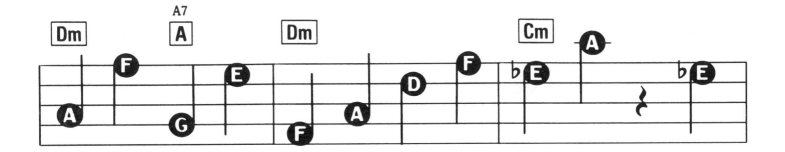

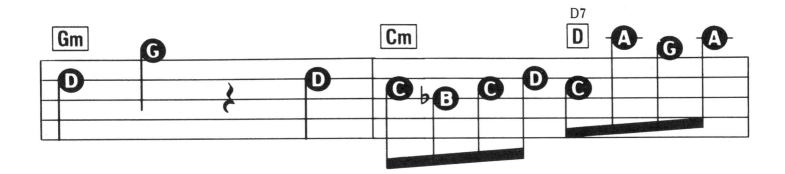

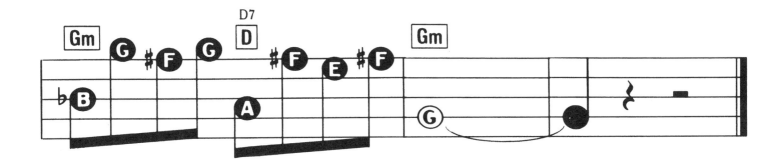

Gavotte
from FRENCH SUITE NO. 5

Registration 8
Rhythm: March or None

By Johann Sebastian Bach

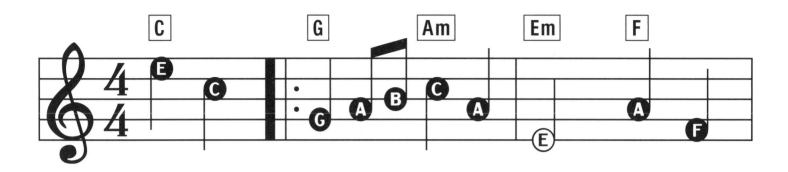

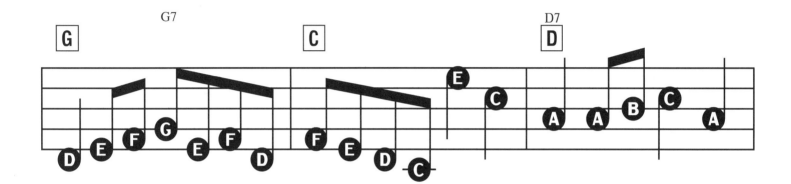

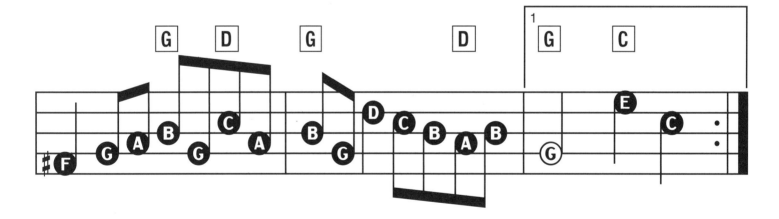

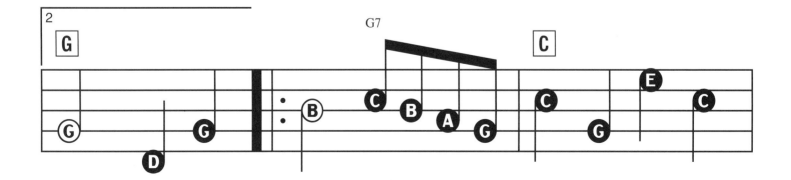

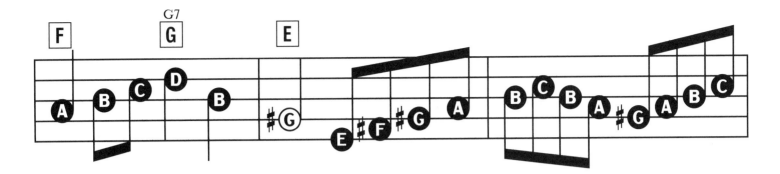

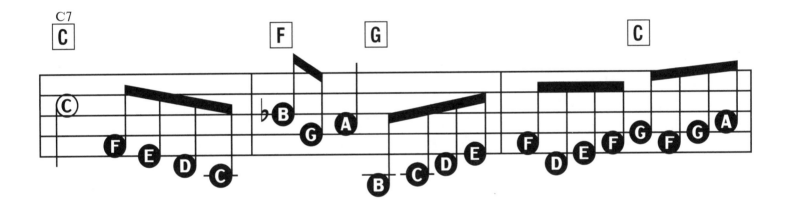

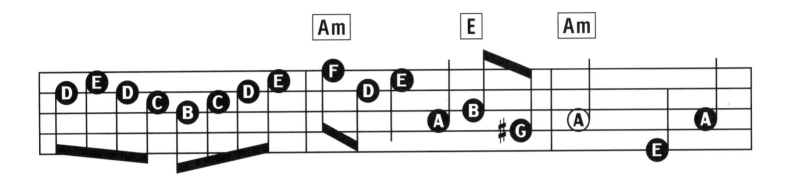

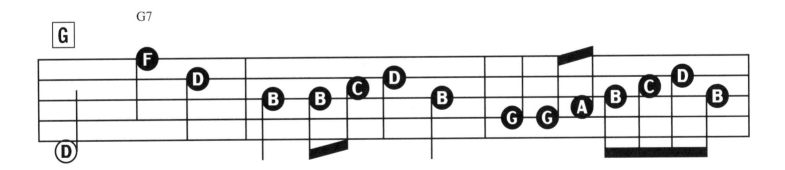

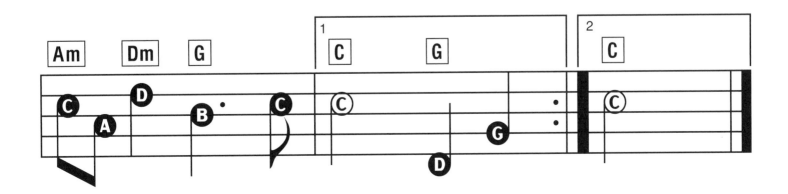

Jesu, Joy of Man's Desiring
from CANTATA NO. 147

Registration 2
Rhythm: None

By Johann Sebastian Bach

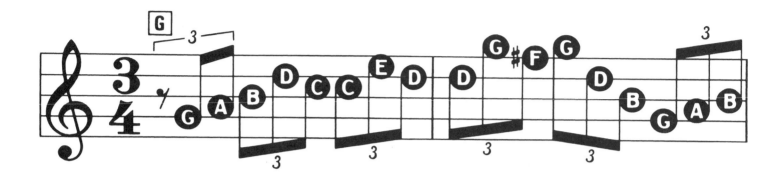

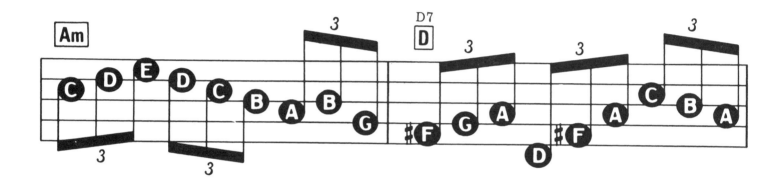

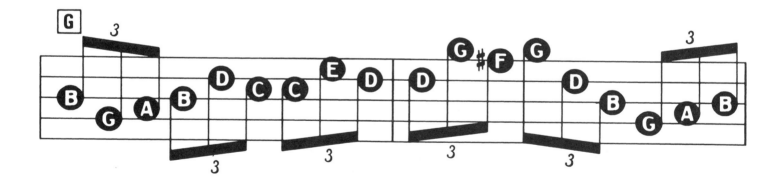

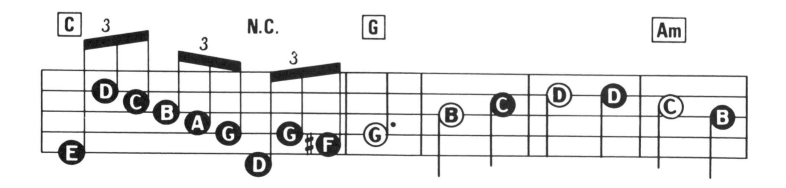

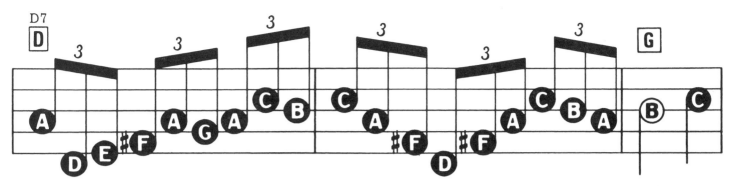

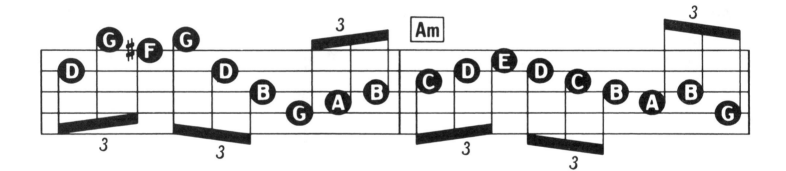

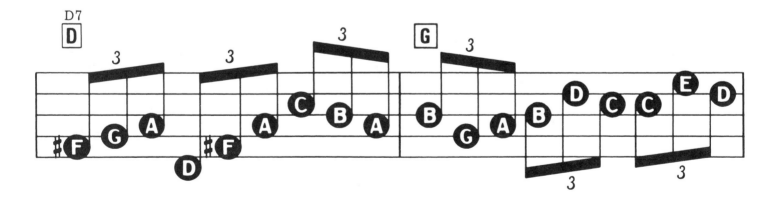

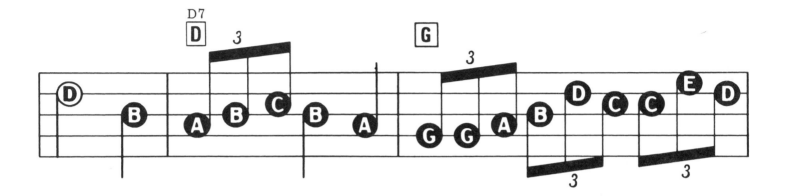

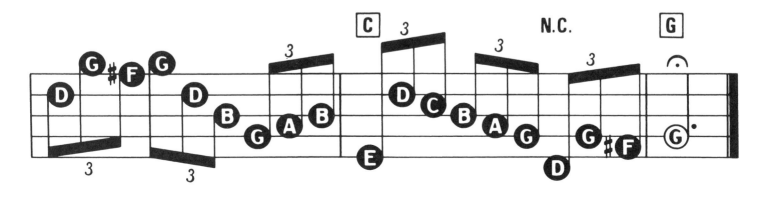

March
from NOTEBOOK FOR ANNA MAGDALENA BACH

Registration 8
Rhythm: March or None

By Johann Sebastian Bach

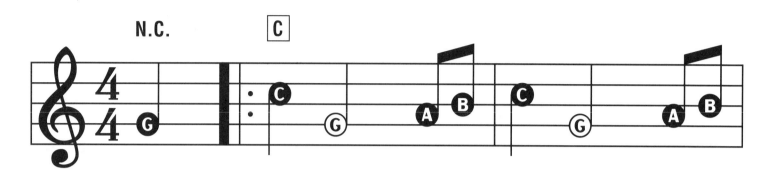

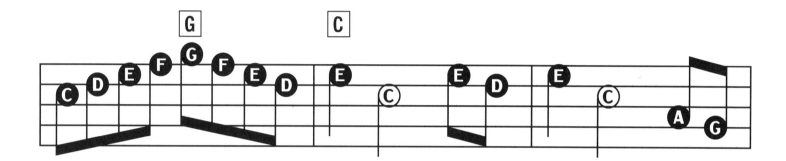

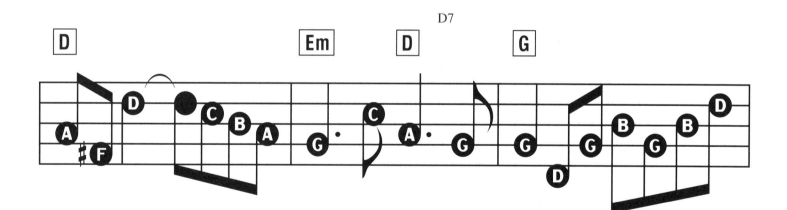

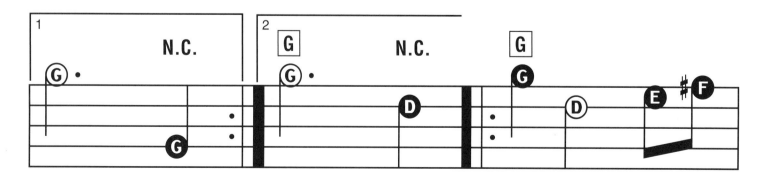

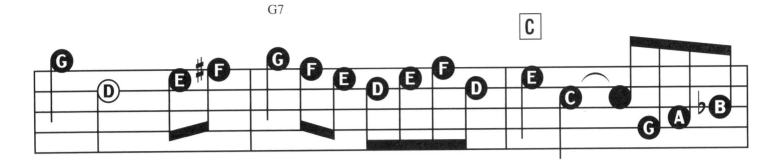

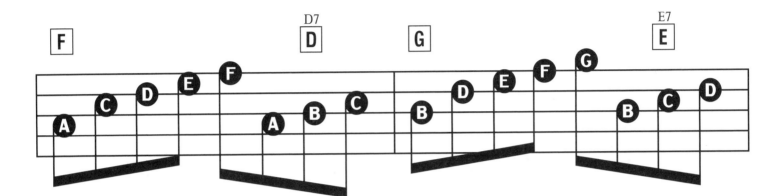

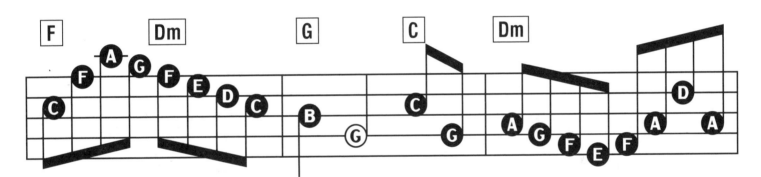

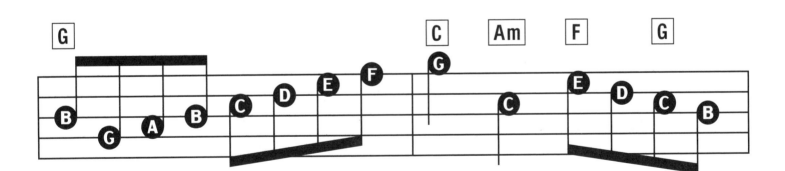

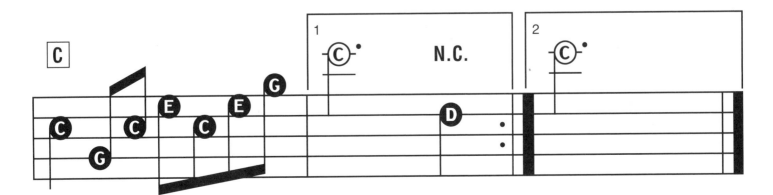

Minuet in G Major
from NOTEBOOK FOR ANNA MAGDALENA BACH

Registration 8
Rhythm: Waltz or None

By Johann Sebastian Bach

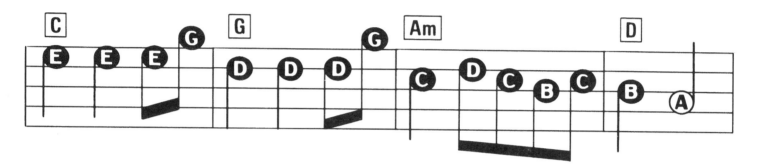

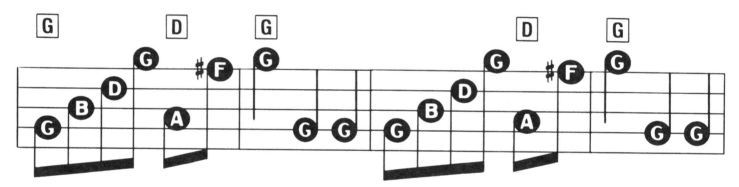

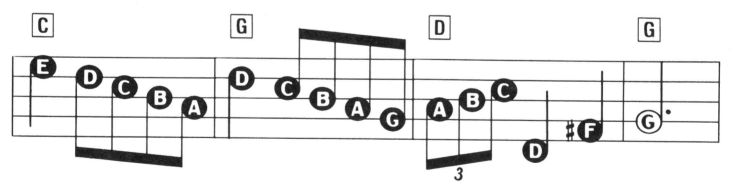

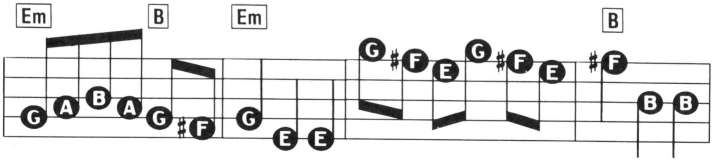

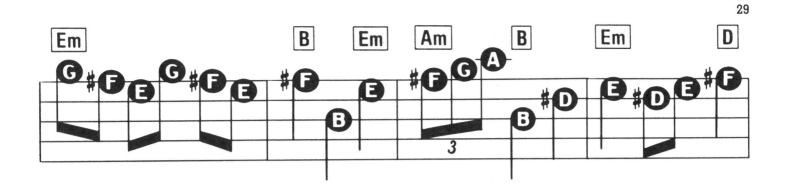
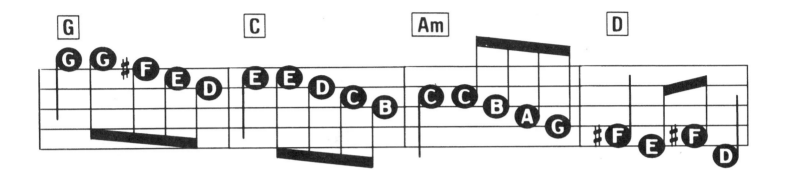
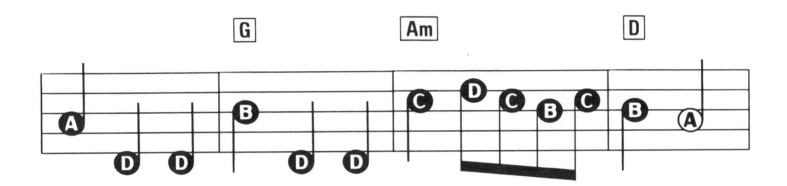
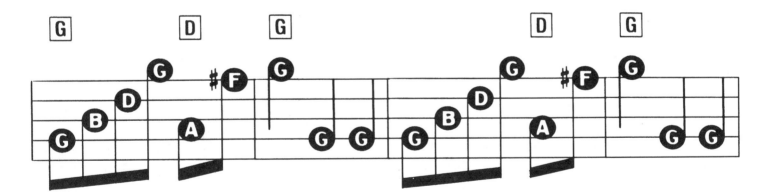
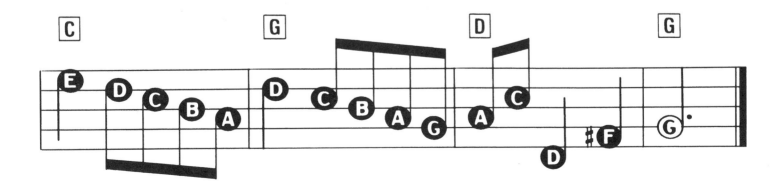

Minuet I in G Major
from NOTEBOOK FOR ANNA MAGDALENA BACH

Registration 8
Rhythm: Waltz

By Johann Sebastian Bach

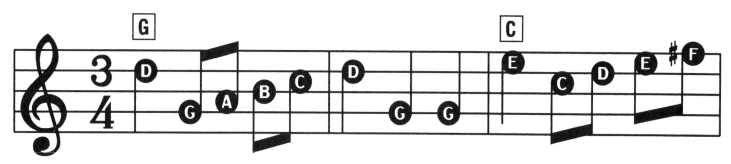

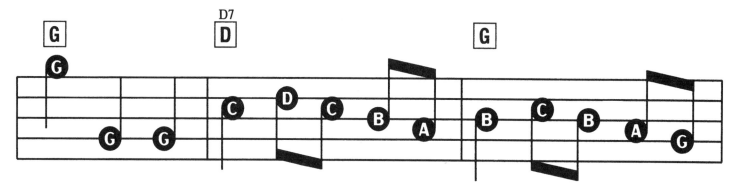

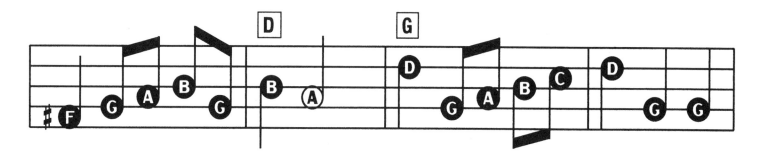

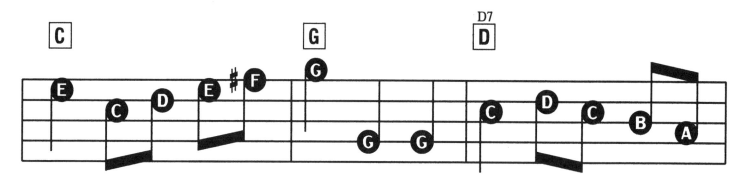

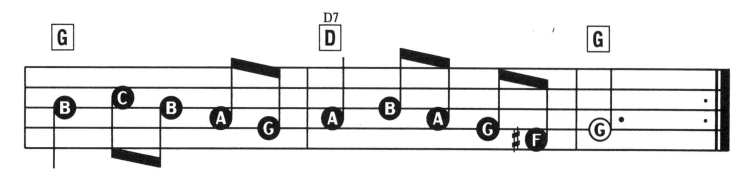

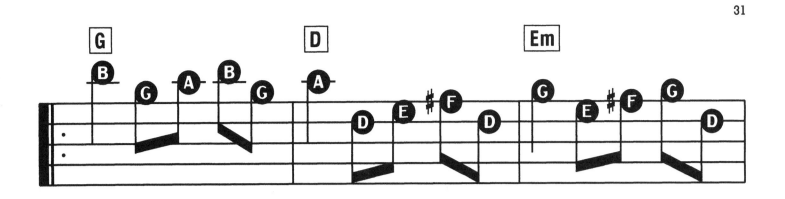

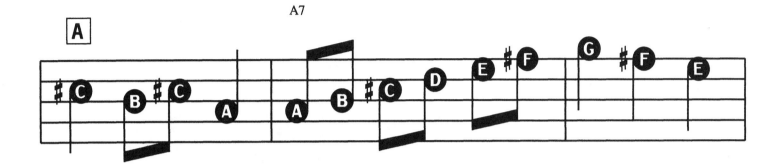

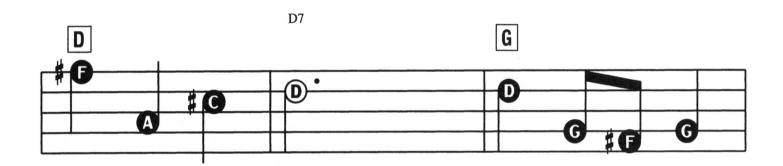

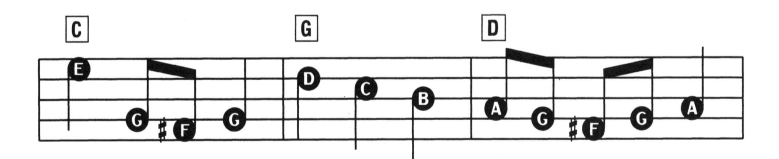

Musette
from NOTEBOOK FOR ANNA MAGDALENA BACH

Registration 8
Rhythm: March

By Johann Sebastian Bach

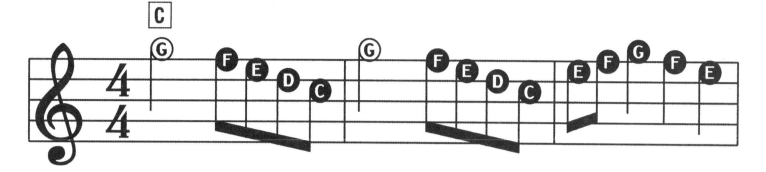

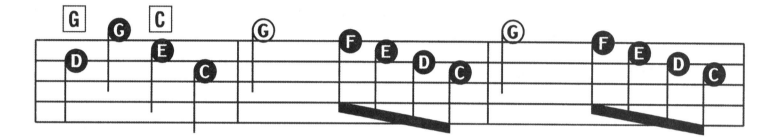

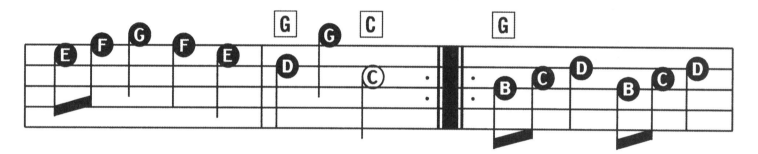

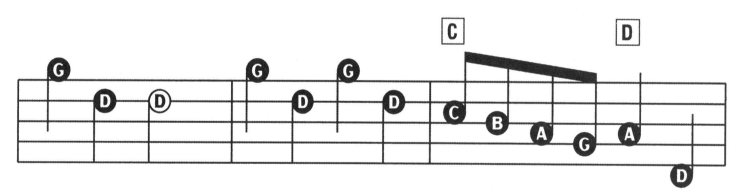

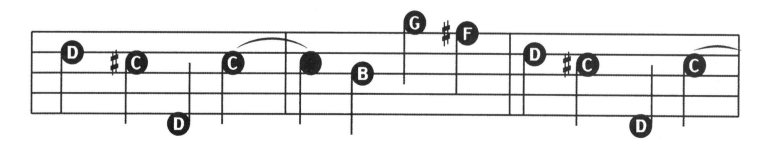

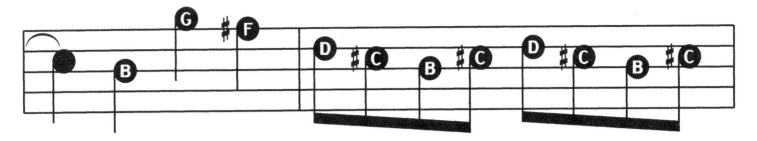

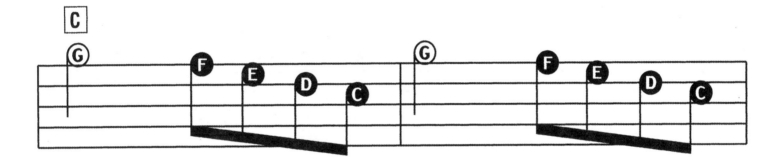

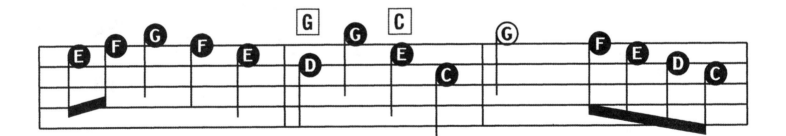

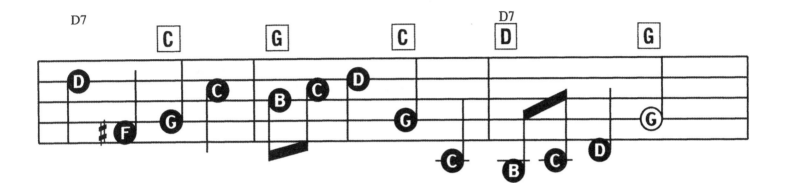

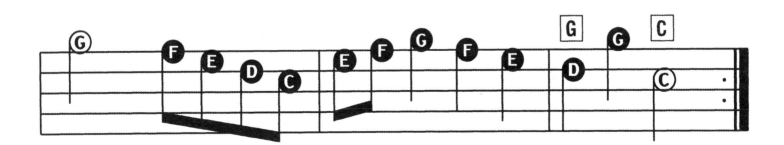

My Heart Ever Faithful
from CANTATA NO. 68

Registration 3
Rhythm: None

By Johann Sebastian Bach

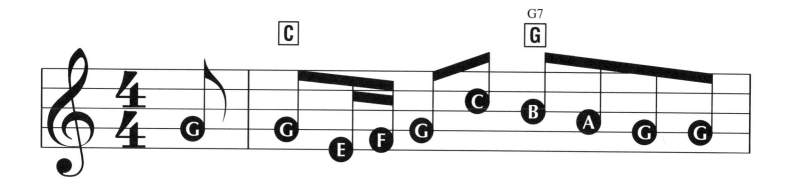

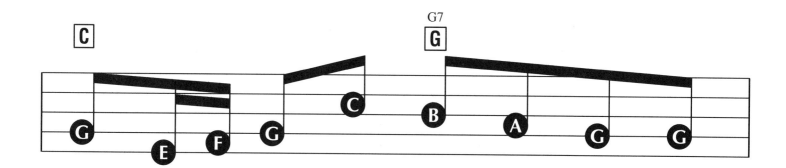

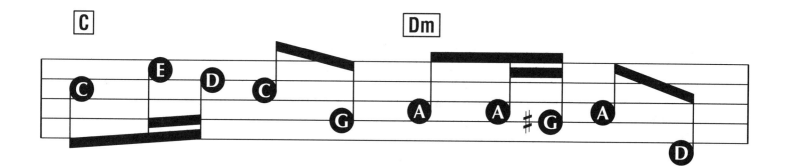

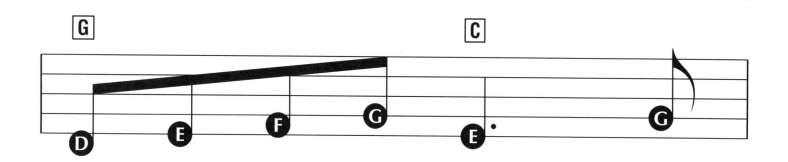

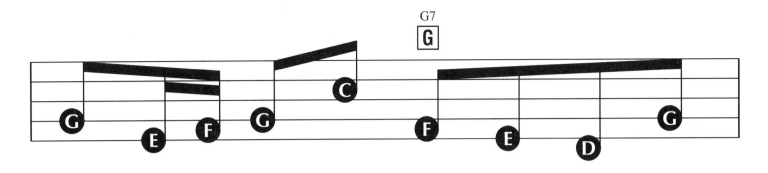

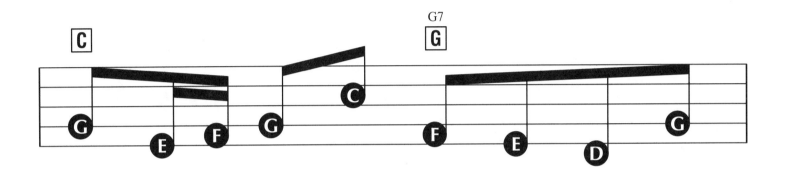

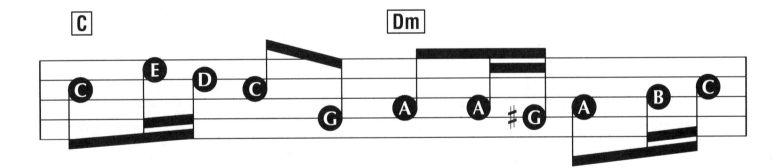

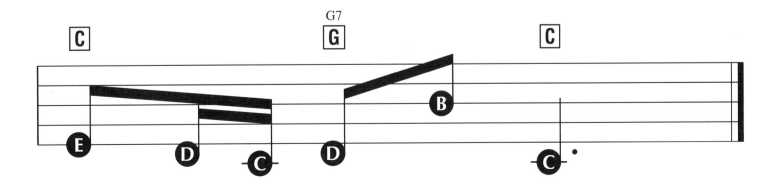

Passion Chorale

Registration 6
Rhythm: None

Words attr. Bernard of Clairvaux
Translated by James W. Alexander
Melody by Hans Leo Hassler
Harmonized by Johann Sebastian Bach

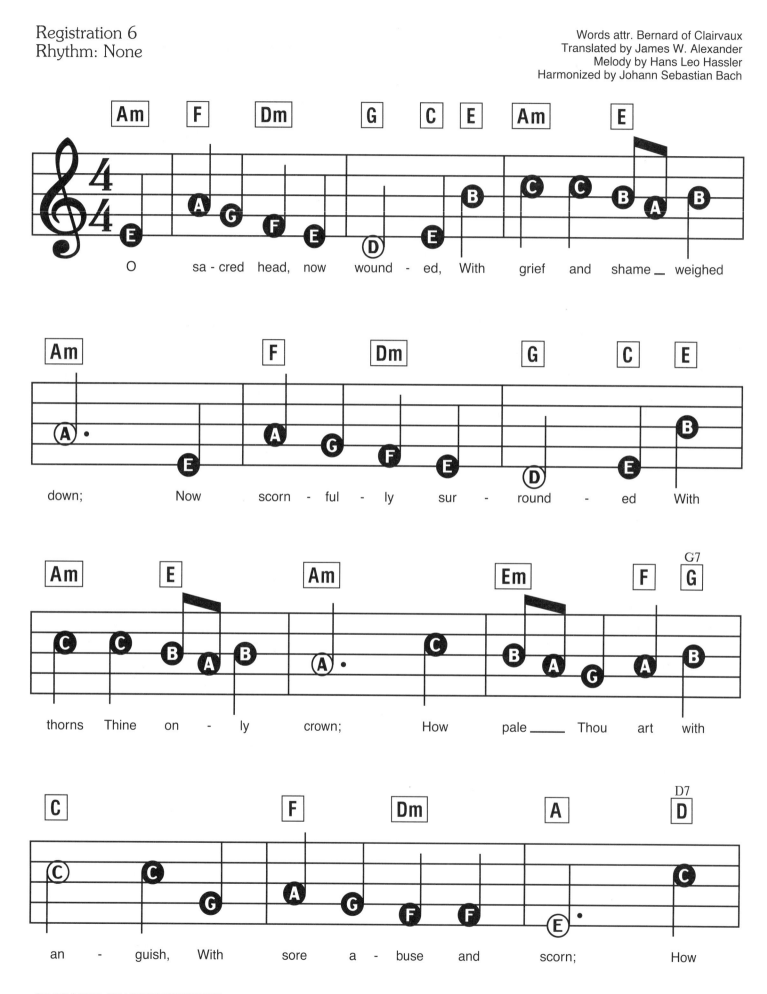

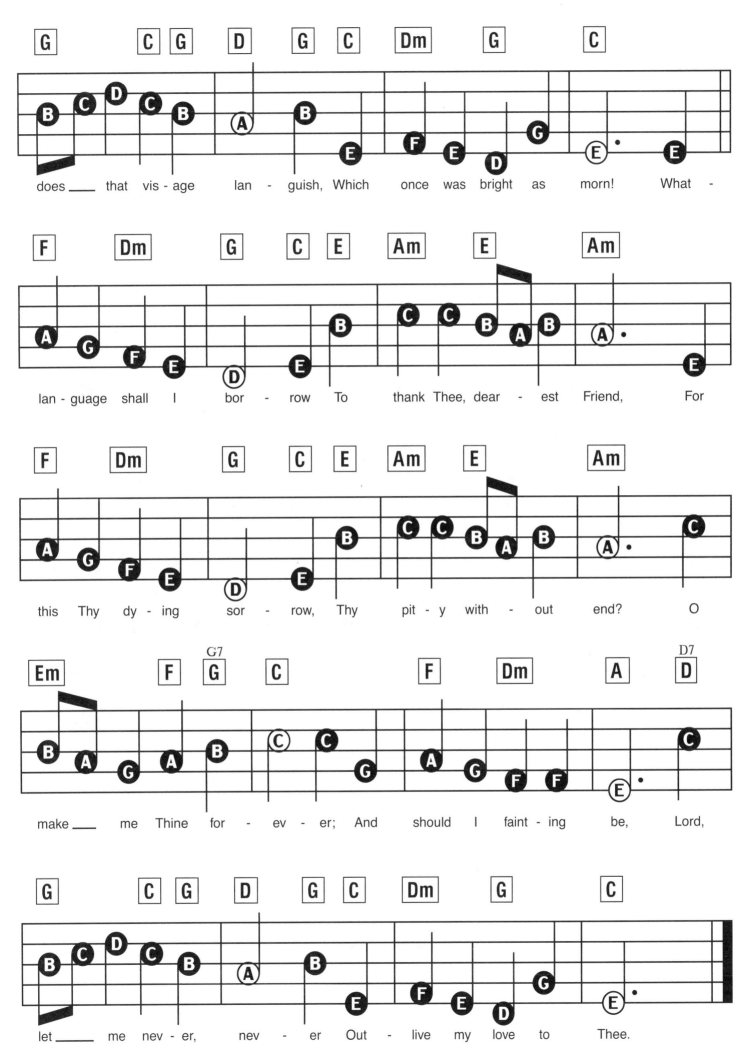

Sheep May Safely Graze
from CANTATA NO. 208

Registration 1
Rhythm: March or None

By Johann Sebastian Bach

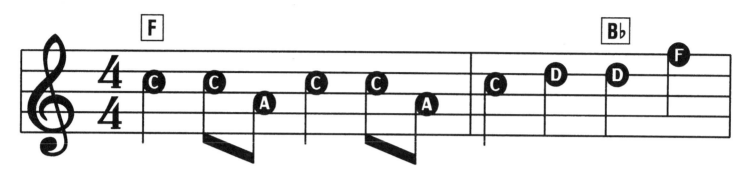

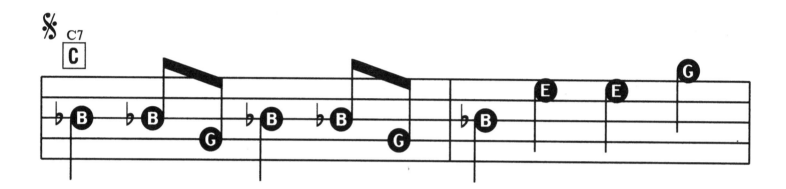

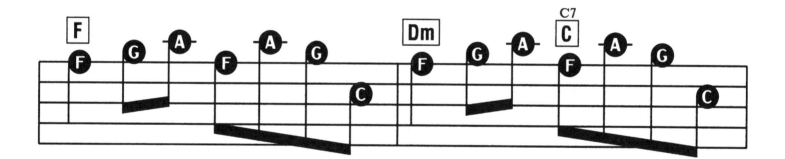

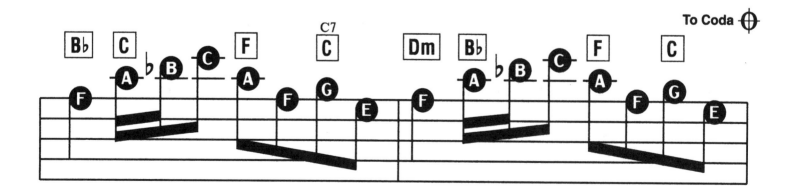

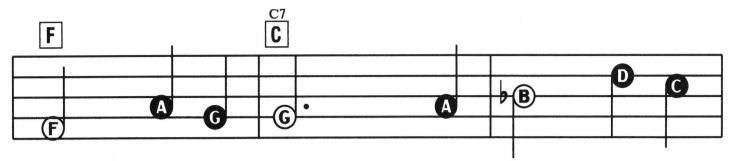

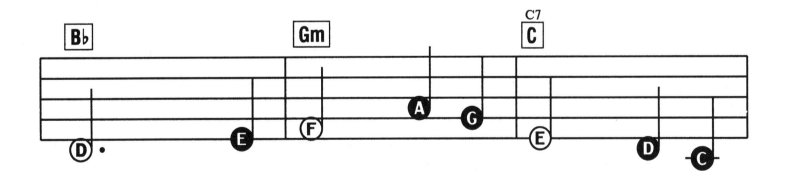

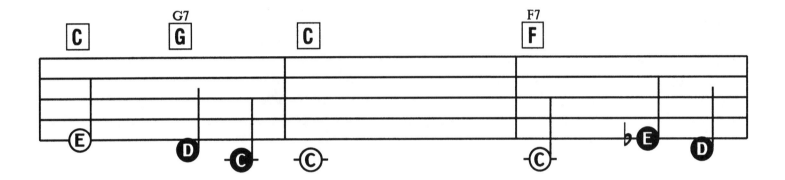

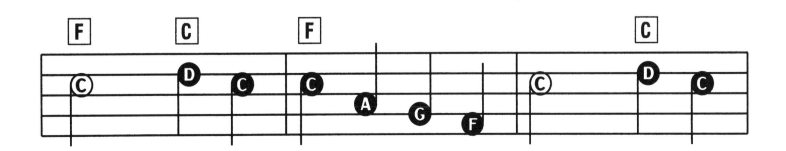

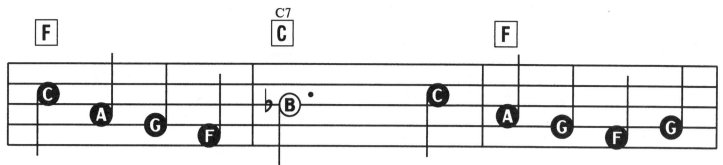

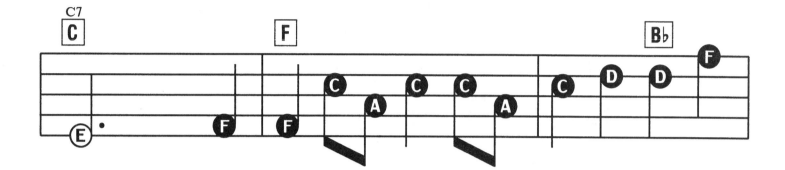

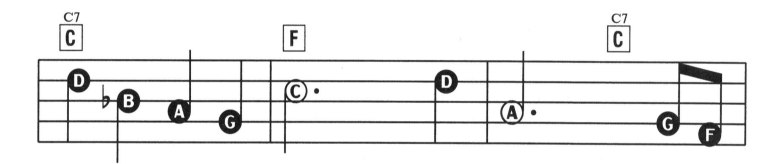

D.S. al Coda
(Return to %
Play to ⊕ and
Skip to Coda)

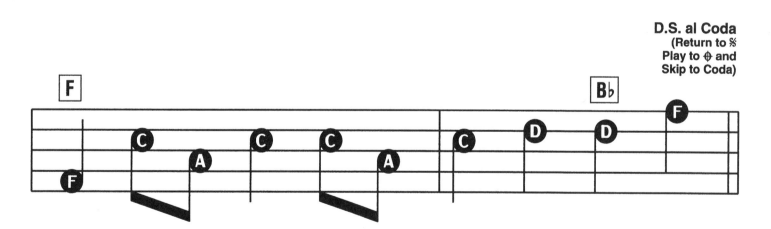

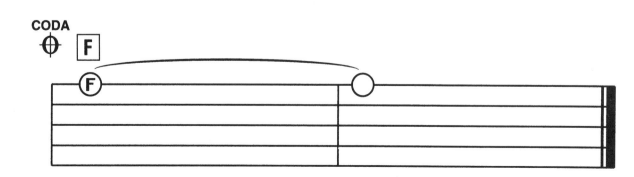

Two-Part Invention in C Major

Registration 8
Rhythm: March or None

By Johann Sebastian Bach

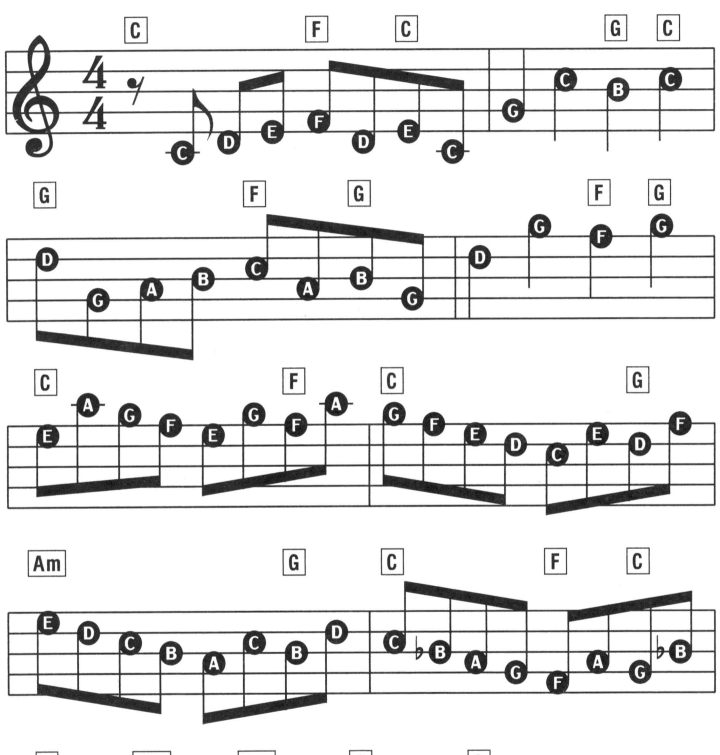

Toccata and Fugue in D Minor

Registration 6
Rhythm: None

By Johann Sebastian Bach

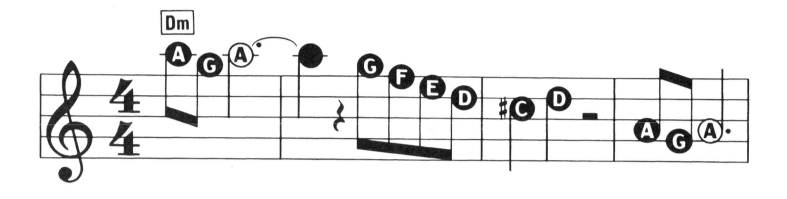

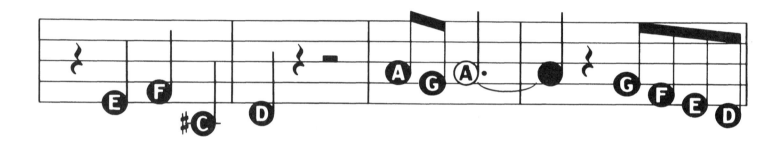

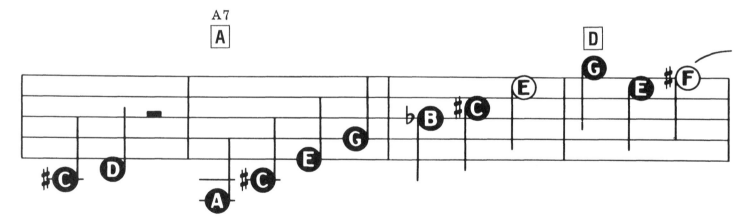

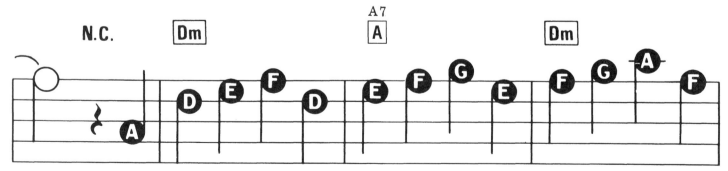

43

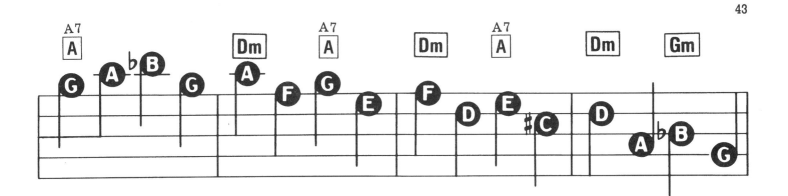
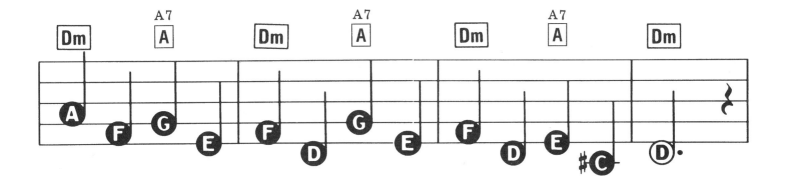
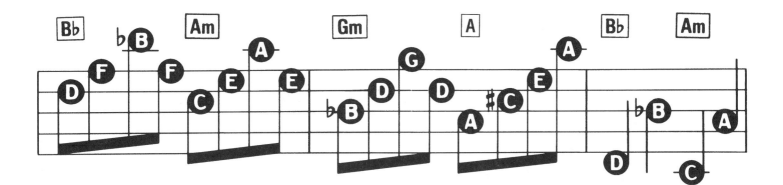
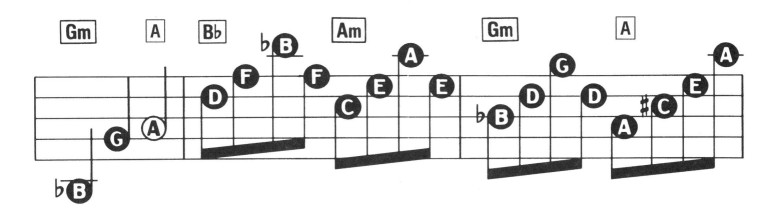
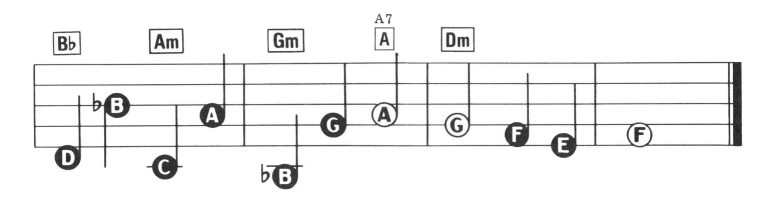

Two-Part Invention in F Major

Registration 8
Rhythm: Waltz or None

By Johann Sebastian Bach

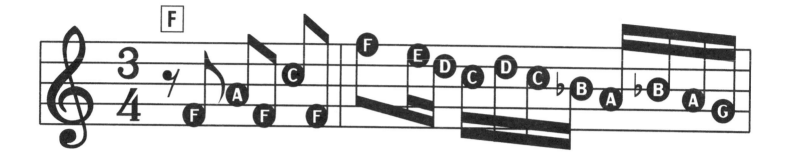

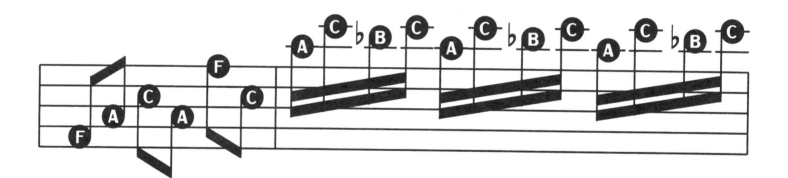

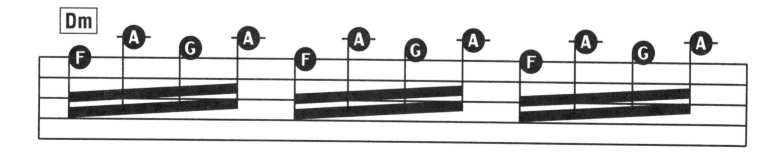

45

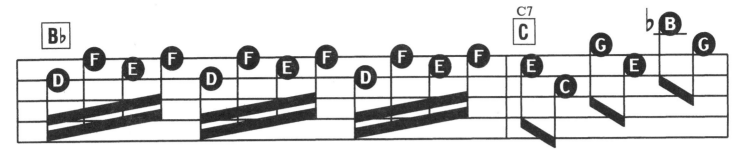

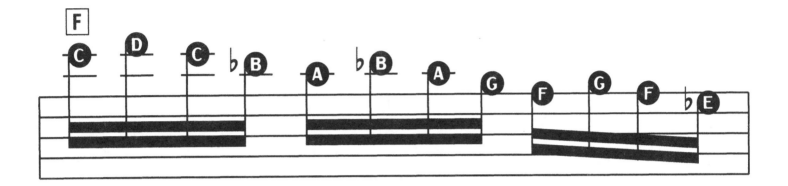

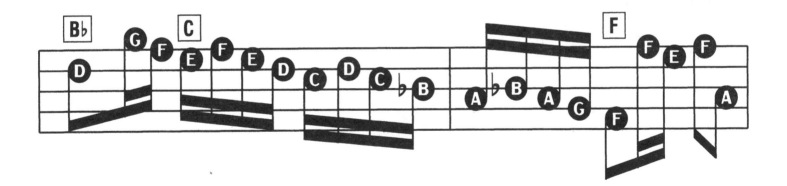

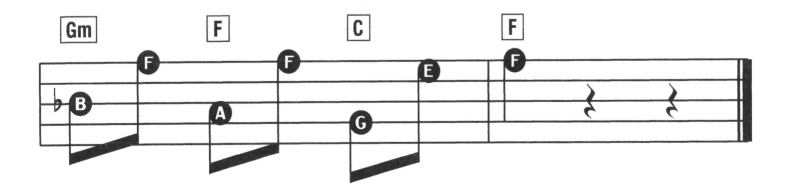

Two-Part Invention in D Minor

Registration 8
Rhythm: Waltz ort None

By Johann Sebastian Bach

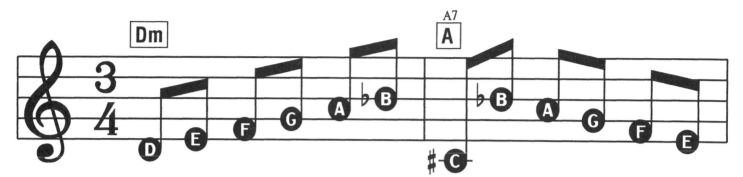

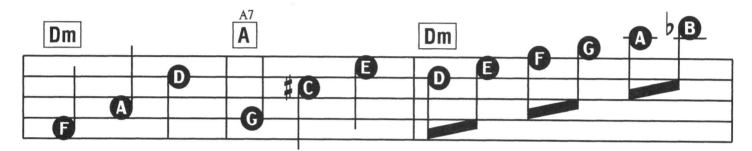

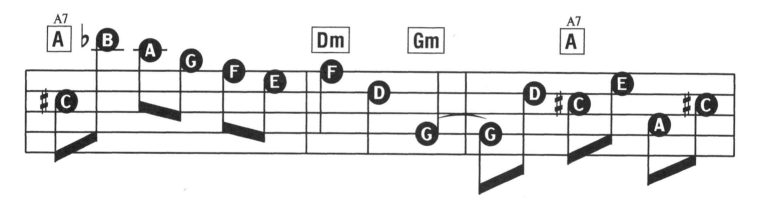

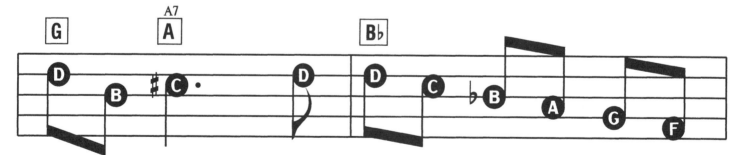

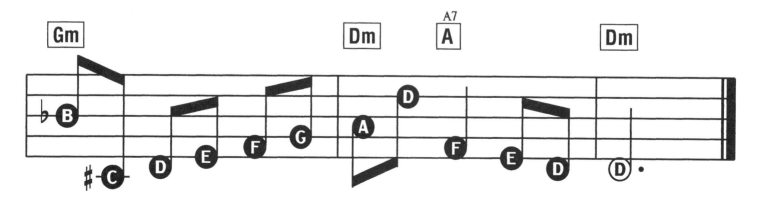

Registration Guide

- Match the Registration number on the song to the corresponding numbered category below. Select and activate an instrumental sound available on your instrument.

- Choose an automatic rhythm appropriate to the mood and style of the song. (Consult your Owner's Guide for proper operation of automatic rhythm features.)

- Adjust the tempo and volume controls to comfortable settings.

Registration

1	Mellow	Flutes, Clarinet, Oboe, Flugel Horn, Trombone, French Horn, Organ Flutes
2	Ensemble	Brass Section, Sax Section, Wind Ensemble, Full Organ, Theater Organ
3	Strings	Violin, Viola, Cello, Fiddle, String Ensemble, Pizzicato, Organ Strings
4	Guitars	Acoustic/Electric Guitars, Banjo, Mandolin, Dulcimer, Ukulele, Hawaiian Guitar
5	Mallets	Vibraphone, Marimba, Xylophone, Steel Drums, Bells, Celesta, Chimes
6	Liturgical	Pipe Organ, Hand Bells, Vocal Ensemble, Choir, Organ Flutes
7	Bright	Saxophones, Trumpet, Mute Trumpet, Synth Leads, Jazz/Gospel Organs
8	Piano	Piano, Electric Piano, Honky Tonk Piano, Harpsichord, Clavi
9	Novelty	Melodic Percussion, Wah Trumpet, Synth, Whistle, Kazoo, Perc. Organ
10	Bellows	Accordion, French Accordion, Mussette, Harmonica, Pump Organ, Bagpipes

FOR ORGANS, PIANOS & ELECTRONIC KEYBOARDS

E-Z PLAY® TODAY PUBLICATIONS

The E-Z Play® Today songbook series is the shortest distance between beginning music and playing fun! Check out this list of highlights and visit www.halleonard.com for a complete listing of all volumes and songlists.

00102278	1. Favorite Songs with 3 Chords	$7.95
00100374	2. Country Sound	$8.95
00100167	3. Contemporary Disney	$16.99
00100382	4. Dance Band Greats	$7.95
00100305	5. All-Time Standards	$7.99
00100428	6. Songs of The Beatles	$10.99
00100442	7. Hits from Musicals	$7.99
00100490	8. Patriotic Songs	$8.99
00100355	9. Christmas Time	$7.95
00100435	10. Hawaiian Songs	$7.95
00110284	12. Star Wars	$7.99
00100248	13. Three-Chord Country Songs	$12.95
00100300	14. All-Time Requests	$8.99
00100370	15. Country Pickin's	$7.95
00100335	16. Broadway's Best	$7.95
00100362	18. Classical Portraits	$7.99
00102277	20. Hymns	$7.95
00100570	22. Sacred Sounds	$7.95
00100214	23. Essential Songs – The 1920s	$16.95
00100206	24. Essential Songs – The 1930s	$16.95
14041364	26. Bob Dylan	$12.99
00001236	27. 60 of the World's Easiest to Play Songs with 3 Chords	$8.95
00101598	28. Fifty Classical Themes	$9.95
00100135	29. Love Songs	$7.95
00100030	30. Country Connection	$8.95
00001289	32. Sing-Along Favorites	$7.95
00100253	34. Inspirational Ballads	$10.95
00102254	35. Frank Sinatra – Romance	$8.95
00100122	36. Good Ol' Songs	$10.95
00100410	37. Favorite Latin Songs	$7.95
00119955	40. Coldplay	$10.99
00100425	41. Songs of Gershwin, Porter & Rodgers	$7.95
00100123	42. Baby Boomers Songbook	$9.95
00100576	43. Sing-along Requests	$8.95
00102135	44. Best of Willie Nelson	$9.99
00100460	45. Love Ballads	$8.99
00100007	47. Duke Ellington – American Composer	$8.95
00100343	48. Gospel Songs of Johnny Cash	$7.95
00100043	49. Elvis, Elvis, Elvis	$9.95
00102114	50. Best of Patsy Cline	$9.95
00100208	51. Essential Songs – The 1950s	$17.95
00100209	52. Essential Songs – The 1960s	$17.95
00100210	53. Essential Songs – The 1970s	$19.95
00100211	54. Essential Songs – The 1980s	$19.95
00100342	55. Johnny Cash	$9.99
00100118	57. More of the Best Songs Ever	$17.99
00100285	58. Four-Chord Songs	$10.99
00100353	59. Christmas Songs	$8.95
00100304	60. Songs for All Occasions	$16.99
00102314	61. Jazz Standards	$10.95
00100409	62. Favorite Hymns	$6.95
00100360	63. Classical Music (Spanish/English)	$7.99
00102223	64. Wicked	$9.95
00100217	65. Hymns with 3 Chords	$7.95
00102312	66. Torch Songs	$14.95
00102218	67. Music from the Motion Picture Ray	$8.95
00100449	69. It's Gospel	$7.95
00100432	70. Gospel Greats	$7.95
00100117	72. Canciones Románticas	$7.99
00100568	75. Sacred Moments	$6.95
00100572	76. The Sound of Music	$8.95
00100489	77. My Fair Lady	$7.99
00100424	81. Frankie Yankovic – Polkas & Waltzes	$7.95
00100286	87. 50 Worship Standards	$14.99
00100287	88. Glee	$9.99
00100577	89. Songs for Children	$7.95
00290104	90. Elton John Anthology	$16.99
00100034	91. 30 Songs for a Better World	$8.95
00100288	92. Michael Bublé – Crazy Love	$10.99
00100036	93. Country Hits	$10.95
00100139	94. Jim Croce – Greatest Hits	$8.95
00100219	95. The Phantom of the Opera (Movie)	$10.95
00100263	96. Mamma Mia – Movie Soundtrack	$7.95
00109768	97. Flower Power	$16.99
00100125	99. Children's Christmas Songs	$7.95
00100602	100. Winter Wonderland	$8.95
00001309	102. Carols of Christmas	$7.99
00119237	103. Two-Chord Songs	$9.99
00100256	107. The Best Praise & Worship Songs Ever	$16.99
00100363	108. Classical Themes (English/Spanish)	$6.95
00102232	109. Motown's Greatest Hits	$12.95
00101566	110. Neil Diamond Collection	$14.99
00100119	111. Season's Greetings	$14.95
00101498	112. Best of The Beatles	$19.95
00100134	113. Country Gospel USA	$10.95
00101612	115. The Greatest Waltzes	$9.95
00100136	118. 100 Kids' Songs	$12.95
00100433	120. Gospel of Bill & Gloria Gaither	$14.95
00100333	121. Boogies, Blues and Rags	$7.95
00100146	122. Songs for Praise & Worship	$8.95
00000001	125. Great Big Book of Children's Songs	$14.99
00101563	127. John Denver's Greatest Hits	$9.95
00116947	128. John Williams	$10.99
00116956	130. Taylor Swift Hits	$10.99
00102318	131. Doo-Wop Songbook	$10.95
00100306	133. Carole King	$9.99
00100171	135. All Around the U.S.A.	$10.95
00001256	136. Christmas Is for Kids	$8.99
00100144	137. Children's Movie Hits	$7.95
00100038	138. Nostalgia Collection	$14.95
00100289	139. Crooners	$19.99
00101956	140. Best of George Strait	$12.95
00100314	142. Classic Jazz	$14.99
00101946	143. The Songs of Paul McCartney	$8.99
00100597	146. Hank Williams – His Best	$7.95
00116916	147. Lincoln	$7.99
00100003	149. Movie Musical Memories	$10.95
00101548	150. Best Big Band Songs Ever	$16.95
00100152	151. Beach Boys – Greatest Hits	$8.95
00101592	152. Fiddler on the Roof	$9.99
00101549	155. Best of Billy Joel	$10.99
00001264	157. Easy Favorites	$7.99
00100315	160. The Grammy Awards Record of the Year 1958-2010	$16.99
00100293	161. Henry Mancini	$9.99
00100049	162. Lounge Music	$10.95
00100295	163. The Very Best of the Rat Pack	$12.99
00101530	164. Best Christmas Songbook	$9.95
00101895	165. Rodgers & Hammerstein Songbook	$9.95
00100148	169. A Charlie Brown Christmas™	$10.99
00101900	170. Kenny Rogers – Greatest Hits	$9.95
00101537	171. Best of Elton John	$7.95
00100321	173. Adele – 21	$10.99
00100149	176. Charlie Brown Collection™	$7.99
00102325	179. Love Songs of The Beatles	$10.99
00101610	181. Great American Country Songbook	$12.95
00001246	182. Amazing Grace	$12.95
00450133	183. West Side Story	$9.99
00100151	185. Carpenters	$10.99
00101606	186. 40 Pop & Rock Song Classics	$12.95
00100155	187. Ultimate Christmas	$17.95
00102276	189. Irish Favorites	$7.95
00100053	191. Jazz Love Songs	$8.95
00101998	192. 65 Standard Hits	$15.95
00123123	193. Bruno Mars	$10.99
00124609	195. Opera Favorites	$8.99
00101609	196. Best of George Gershwin	$14.99
00100057	198. Songs in 3/4 Time	$9.95
00119857	199. Jumbo Songbook	$24.99
00101539	200. Best Songs Ever	$19.95
00101540	202. Best Country Songs Ever	$17.95
00101541	203. Best Broadway Songs Ever	$17.99
00101542	204. Best Easy Listening Songs Ever	$17.95
00101543	205. Best Love Songs Ever	$17.95
00100058	208. Easy Listening Favorites	$7.95
00100059	210. '60s Pop Rock Hits	$12.95
14041777	211. The Big Book of Nursery Rhymes & Children's Songs	$12.99
00126895	212. Frozen	$9.99
00101546	213. Disney Classics	$14.95
00101533	215. Best Christmas Songs Ever	$19.95
00100156	219. Christmas Songs with 3 Chords	$8.99
00102080	225. Lawrence Welk Songbook	$9.95
00101931	228. Songs of the '20s	$13.95
00101932	229. Songs of the '30s	$13.95
00101933	230. Songs of the '40s	$14.95
00101935	232. Songs of the '60s	$14.95
00101936	233. Songs of the '70s	$14.95
00101581	235. Elvis Presley Anthology	$15.99
00290170	239. Big Book of Children's Songs	$14.95
00290120	240. Frank Sinatra	$14.95
00100158	243. Oldies! Oldies! Oldies!	$10.95
00290242	244. Songs of the '80s	$14.95
00100041	245. Best of Simon & Garfunkel	$8.95
00100269	247. Essential Songs – Broadway	$17.99
00100296	248. The Love Songs of Elton John	$12.99
00100175	249. Elvis – 30 #1 Hits	$9.95
00102113	251. Phantom of the Opera (Broadway)	$14.95
00100301	255. Four-Chord Hymns	$8.95
00100203	256. Very Best of Lionel Richie	$8.95
00100302	258. Four-Chord Worship	$9.99
00100178	259. Norah Jones – Come Away with Me	$9.95
00102306	261. Best of Andrew Lloyd Webber	$12.95
00100063	266. Latin Hits	$7.95
00100062	269. Love That Latin Beat	$7.95
00100179	270. Christian Christmas Songbook	$14.95
00101425	272. ABBA Gold – Greatest Hits	$7.95
00102248	275. Classical Hits – Bach, Beethoven & Brahms	$6.95
00100186	277. Stevie Wonder – Greatest Hits	$9.95
00100237	280. Dolly Parton	$9.99
00100068	283. Best Jazz Standards Ever	$15.95
00100244	287. Josh Groban	$10.95
00100022	288. Sing-a-Long Christmas	$10.95
00100023	289. Sing-a-Long Christmas Carols	$9.95
00102124	293. Movie Classics	$9.95
00100069	294. Old Fashioned Love Songs	$9.95
00100303	295. Best of Michael Bublé	$12.99
00100075	296. Best of Cole Porter	$7.95
00102130	298. Beautiful Love Songs	$7.95
00001102	301. Kid's Songfest	$9.99
00102147	306. Irving Berlin Collection	$14.95
00102182	308. Greatest American Songbook	$9.99
00100194	309. 3-Chord Rock 'n' Roll	$8.95
00001580	311. The Platters Anthology	$7.95
02501515	312. Barbra – Love Is the Answer	$10.99
00100196	314. Chicago	$8.95
00100197	315. VH1's 100 Greatest Songs of Rock & Roll	$19.95
00100080	322. Dixieland	$7.95
00100277	325. Taylor Swift	$10.99
00100082	327. Tonight at the Lounge	$7.95
00100092	333. Great Gospel Favorites	$7.95
00100278	338. The Best Hymns Ever	$19.99
00100279	340. Anthology of Jazz Songs	$19.99
00100280	341. Anthology of Rock Songs	$19.99
00100281	342. Anthology of Broadway Songs	$19.99
00100282	343. Anthology of Love Songs	$19.99
00100283	344. Anthology of Latin Songs	$19.99
00100284	345. Anthology of Movie Songs	$19.99
00102235	346. Big Book of Christmas Songs	$14.95
00100292	347. Anthology of Country Songs	$19.99
00100095	359. 100 Years of Song	$17.95
00100096	360. More 100 Years of Song	$19.95
00100103	375. Songs of Bacharach & David	$7.95
00100107	392. Disney Favorites	$19.95
00100108	393. Italian Favorites	$7.95
00100111	394. Best Gospel Songs Ever	$17.95
00100114	398. Disney's Princess Collections	$10.99
00100115	400. Classical Masterpieces	$10.95

HAL•LEONARD® CORPORATION

7777 W. BLUEMOUND RD. P.O. BOX 13819 MILWAUKEE, WI 53213

Prices, contents, and availability subject to change without notice.

0714